THE THREE MILE ISLAND
NUCLEAR DISASTER

Essential Events

The Three Mile Island
Nuclear Disaster

BY MARCIA AMIDON LUSTED

Content Consultant
Dr. Craig M. Marianno,
Nuclear Security Science and Policy Institute
Texas A&M University

ABDO
Publishing Company

6119572096

2742987

363.1799

L

CREDITS

Published by ABDO Publishing Company, PO Box 398166,
Minneapolis, MN 55439. Copyright © 2012 by Abdo Consulting
Group, Inc. International copyrights reserved in all countries.
No part of this book may be reproduced in any form without
written permission from the publisher. The Essential Library™
is a trademark and logo of ABDO Publishing Company.

Printed in the United States of America,
North Mankato, Minnesota
092011
012012

 THIS BOOK CONTAINS AT LEAST 10% RECYCLED MATERIALS.

Editor: Angela Wiechmann
Copy Editor: Chelsea Whitcomb
Cover design: Marie Tupy
Interior design and production: Kazuko Collins

Library of Congress Cataloging-in-Publication Data
Lusted, Marcia Amidon.
  The Three Mile Island nuclear disaster / by Marcia Amidon
Lusted.
      p. cm. -- (Essential events)
  Includes bibliographical references and index.
  ISBN 978-1-61783-311-3
  1. Three Mile Island Nuclear Power Plant (Pa.)--Juvenile
literature. 2. Nuclear power plants--Accidents--Pennsylvania-
-Harrisburg Region--Juvenile literature. 3. Nuclear energy--
Juvenile literature. I. Title.
  TK1345.H37L87 2012
  363.17'990974818--dc23
                              2011036182

TABLE OF CONTENTS

Dusk falls on a quiet evening before the March 28, 1979, accident at the Three Mile Island plant.

MARCH 28, 1979

At approximately 4:00 a.m. on March 28, 1979, a loud roar startled Holly Garnish awake. "Picture the biggest jet at an airport and the noise it makes," she later said. "That's what I heard. It shook the windows, the whole house."[1] Holly eventually went back to sleep. The sound of the power plant venting steam was not unusual to those who lived close to the Three Mile Island Nuclear Power Plant (TMI) near Middletown, Pennsylvania, run by Metropolitan Edison Company, or Met-Ed. But Holly and other residents of the area had no way of knowing this was not a routine steam vent at the Three Mile Island plant.

The plant consisted of two nuclear reactors, TMI-1 and TMI-2. TMI-1 was offline for refueling, but TMI-2 was running at full power. But around 4:00 a.m., a feedwater system that pumped water to the steam generator malfunctioned. It shut off the flow. This was serious because water needed to flow into the steam generator to replace the steam flowing out to the turbine and creating electricity. Without that supply of water, the plant's nuclear reactor could overheat.

Statistics Snapshot

In the United States today, there are 104 operating nuclear power plants located in 31 states. They generate 20 percent of the country's electricity. In seven states, nuclear energy produces more electricity than any other source. Vermont gets more of its electricity (72 percent) from nuclear power than any other state. The oldest operating nuclear plant in the country began running in 1969, and the newest began operating in 1996.

THE FIRST ALARMS

As soon as the feedwater pump malfunctioned, it triggered more than 100 alarms in the TMI-2 control room. The control room is the brain of a nuclear power plant. In it, operators can monitor and control every aspect of the plant's operation. As writer Mike Gray described it in the PBS film *Meltdown at Three Mile Island*,

> *Within minutes, the control room console went wild. Hundreds of lights started flashing, accompanied by piercing horns and sirens. One operator recalled that the console was "lit up like a Christmas tree."*[2]

The alarms were also due to an auxiliary source of cooling water that should have started automatically, but did not. Critical valves controlling the flow of this water had been left closed during a maintenance test, which was strictly against the policies

Inside the Control Room

In the presidential commission's report on the events at Three Mile Island, there is a description of what it was like to enter the control room there: "To a casual visitor, the control room at TMI-2 can be an intimidating place, with messages coming from the loudspeaker of the plant's paging system; panel upon panel of red, green, amber, and white lights; and alarms that sound or flash warnings many times each hour. Reactor operators are trained how to respond and to respond quickly in emergencies. Initial actions are ingrained, almost automatic and unthinking."[3]

Inside the Three Mile Island control room

of the Nuclear Regulatory Commission (NRC).
Without this emergency water, the steam generator
would completely boil away the remaining water, and
the reactor's temperature and pressure would rise
rapidly.

However, other parts of the plant's emergency
system worked exactly as they were designed.
The turbine shut down automatically, and steam
began flowing into a collecting tank. The plant
"scrammed," which means the reactor automatically
shut down so the nuclear reaction would stop.

Pressure decreased in the reactor system. But then another malfunction occurred. After the pressure decreased, the regulating valve should have closed, but it got stuck. The plant's operators had no way of knowing the valve was still open. They did not know water that should have been cooling the reactor was now flowing out through the stuck-open valve.

FALSE SIGNALS AND FALSE STEPS

Again, some of the plant's emergency systems did what they were supposed to do. The emergency core cooling system, which was another supply of water to keep the reactor from overheating, started automatically when the water pressure fell too low. But the plant operators were now bombarded with hundreds of alarms and flashing lights from the control panel. They were trying to assess what was happening, based on their experience and training. One operator misread information about the flow of water into the reactor, thinking there was enough. According to an article in the *Washington Post*:

> *"He thought he saw fluid rising in the pressurizer, suggesting that the reactor vessel was still filling with the water. So he thinks, 'Ah, ha. I've got the system full of water; any*

more I pump in there is just going to spill on the floor,'"

NRC source said. "Big mistake!" What was really happening was that pressure was still plunging, water was still flashing into steam, and water levels inside the reactor vessel were in fact dropping.[4]

Over the next hour, the water levels inside the reactor core kept dropping. That exposed more and more of the reactor's fuel rods, causing the fuel to overheat and melt. Radioactive gases escaped into the cooling system and then leaked into the reactor building through the stuck-open valve. Radioactive water was also spilling from a containment tank into the auxiliary building until it was several feet deep on the floor. High radiation alarms began sounding. Shortly before 7:00 a.m., a site emergency was declared at the Three Mile Island plant. A siren

An Invisible Accident

Theodore Gross, a Pennsylvania State University administrator, would later tell a presidential commission about the toll the TMI accident took on local people: "Never before have people been asked to live with such ambiguity. The TMI accident—an accident we cannot see or taste or smell . . . is an accident that is invisible. I think the fact that it is invisible creates a sense of uncertainty and fright on the part of people that may well go beyond the reality of the accident itself."[5]

wailed, telling workers to evacuate critical areas of the plant. Shortly after, a general site emergency was called because of radiation levels.

By 8:25 a.m., the first news of the emergency reached the general public. Mike Pintek, news director at the local WKBO radio station, had just finished playing a pop song when he announced, "There is a general emergency at Metropolitan Edison Company's Three Mile Island nuclear power plant. A utility spokesman says there is a problem with a feed-water pump."[6] He added that there was no danger to the general public.

At 9:06 a.m., the story spread nationwide when the Associated Press announced, "Officials at the Three Mile Island Nuclear plant have declared a 'general emergency,' a state police spokesman said today."[7] It was enough to bring hundreds of reporters from local, national, and international news media to Three Mile Island.

Media Madhouse

It is estimated that more than 300 journalists from television networks and newspapers came to the TMI area to report on the accident. They came from all over the United States, as well as from Canada, England, West Germany, Japan, France, Australia, Switzerland, Denmark, and Sweden.

As the events at Three Mile Island unfolded over the course of several tense days, there would be much confusion, mis-communication, and conflicting information about what was really happening and what the dangers were. Ultimately, the incident at Three Mile Island would show that most of the plant's emergency systems and procedures worked as they should have and that there were no measurable long-term health effects for the general public. But it was still the worst nuclear accident in

Met-Ed's Version

In the PBS documentary *Meltdown at Three Mile Island*, former Pennsylvania Governor Richard Thornburgh commented on how Met-Ed painted its own version of the accident:

They said that everything was under control. It wasn't. They said that all of the response mechanisms at the plant had worked properly. They hadn't, but generally, the impression was left that there really wasn't much room for concern. MetEd had omitted some very vital information—that there had been an uncontrolled release of radiation from the plant. And so, while we had no reason to suspect at the time that there was anything missing in their characterization of it, we still set about to go to look to other sources to try to verify and check out. . . . The first thing that eroded our willingness to accept the utility's characterization of the event was learning that this uncontrolled release of radiation had taken place. That was a very substantial bit of information that they had neglected to share with the public at their press conference on the morning of the accident. They said they hadn't been asked about it, but it seemed to us that it was incumbent upon them to come forward with that.[8]

US history. March 28, 1979, would be a pivotal day, shaping the future of the nuclear industry, as well as Americans' attitudes toward nuclear power. Decades later, its impact can still be felt. ⌐

A view inside the Three Mile Island nuclear reactor

President Dwight Eisenhower, center, speaks to cabinet members about the Atoms for Peace program.

Nuclear Power in the United States

Before the construction of Three Mile Island and other similar plants, the United States had a long history of experimenting with nuclear power. The United States had already used the nuclear fission process in the atom bomb.

This was the type of bomb dropped on Japan at the end of World War II (1939–1945). After the war, the military also experimented with developing a nuclear-powered airplane, as well as ships and submarines powered by nuclear reactors. During the Cold War between the United States and the former Soviet Union, military uses for nuclear power seemed to be the highest priority. This worried many people, including scientists who wanted to see a worldwide movement for peaceful uses of nuclear power. As early as 1945, a nuclear physicist named Alvin Weinberg told the US Senate's Special Committee on Atomic Energy,

Atomic power can cure as well as kill. It can fertilize and enrich a region as well as devastate it. It can widen a man's horizons as well as force him back into the cave.[1]

In 1953, President Dwight D. Eisenhower gave his famous Atoms

Walt Disney

In 1956, Walt Disney, founder of the Walt Disney Company, opened an exhibit in the Tomorrowland section of his Disneyland amusement park in California. It showcased atomic energy for cheerful, nondestructive uses. It also showed the history of atomic research and how atomic reactors could provide power for the entire world. Disney also published a companion children's book and made an *Our Friend the Atom* film for his weekly television show. He wanted to show the public, and especially children, that science could lead humans in peaceful directions, too.

for Peace speech about the growth of nuclear weapons and the future of the world. He said,

This greatest of destructive forces can be developed into a great boon, for the benefit of all mankind. The United States knows that peaceful power from atomic energy is no dream of the future. The capability, already proved, is here today. [2]

THE FIRST POWER PLANTS

The first countries to build nuclear power plants for producing energy in the 1950s were

---

The Plowshares Program

After World War II, many scientists, politicians, and citizens wanted to see nuclear power used for more than just bombs and other military uses. The Atomic Energy Commission (AEC) established the Plowshares Program as a way to promote nonmilitary uses for nuclear power. The program got its name from a biblical phrase about turning swords (weapons) into plowshares (a peaceful farming tool).

Between 1958 and 1975, the Plowshares Program explored ways to use nuclear energy for large-scale excavating, quarrying, and underground engineering. The program participants felt that nuclear energy could be used in place of traditional explosives to construct canals, harbors, railway tunnels, and underground storage reservoirs. They considered projects such as Project Chariot, which would have excavated a harbor and ship basin on the northwest coast of Alaska. Project Carryall would have blasted a railway pass in the Bristol Mountains of California. There was even an idea to blast a canal in Central America. All of these projects would have used nuclear explosions, rather than dynamite or other traditional explosives, for excavating. However, these projects never actually happened because they were too expensive. There was also the fear that radioactive fallout from the explosions would drift into populated areas.

the Soviet Union and the United Kingdom. In 1957, the United States opened its first nuclear power plant in Shippingport, Pennsylvania, which generated electricity for the city of Pittsburgh and its surrounding areas. The reactor for the Shippingport plant had originally been built for a nuclear-powered aircraft carrier. Eisenhower's administration decided instead to use it to help the United States catch up with other countries using nuclear power for electricity. Eisenhower also wanted to show that the country could use atomic energy in peaceful ways. Writer Robert Martin describes the dramatic ceremony that took place in September 1953 when the Shippingport plant was ready to run:

> Ground was broken . . . in dramatic fashion with the wave of an "Atomic Wand" from President Eisenhower over a Geiger Counter that was used to send a signal over a telephone line to an unmanned bulldozer positioned to dig. On December 23, 1957, less than four and a half years after the construction contract had been signed, the Shippingport nuclear power plant reached full power and was providing electricity to Pittsburgh.[3]

After the construction of Shippingport, nuclear power plants were built all over the country. Leading vendors General Electric and Westinghouse competed to sell nuclear power plants to utility companies that provided energy to consumers. For a fixed price, the vendors would build nuclear plants that were ready to operate. During the 1970s and 1980s, almost 100 new nuclear plants began operating in the United States.

THE ENERGY CRISIS

A major reason why nuclear power plants were so attractive in the 1970s was the energy crisis. Before 1973, most Americans could not imagine they would ever run out of energy for electricity and automobiles. But as Americans began using more and more energy in the 1970s, US oil producers could no longer keep up. Americans began importing their oil from other countries, and demand continued climbing. Then in October 1973, the Organization of Petroleum Exporting Countries

Newest Plants

Although no new nuclear plants have been approved in the United States since the 1979 Three Mile Island accident, the following list features the newest plants licensed for operation. These plants were already in the construction process when the TMI accident occurred.

- February 1996: Watts Bar 1 in Tennessee
- April 1993: Comanche Peak 2 in Texas
- April 1990: Comanche Peak 1 in Texas
- March 1990: Seabrook 1 in New Hampshire
- August 1989: Limerick 2 in Pennsylvania

Technicians oversee the construction of the reactor at the Shippingport
nuclear power plant, the first in the United States.

(OPEC) in the Middle East began restricting the
amount of oil it sold to the United States. This
created shortages of oil and gasoline and made prices
rise sharply. Suddenly, people had to line up at gas
stations, often only to discover the stations had run
out of gasoline. Many Americans bought smaller
cars and paid more attention to how much energy

they used. Nuclear energy seemed more attractive, which resulted in the construction of more nuclear plants.

THREE MILE ISLAND

The first Three Mile Island plant, referred to as TMI-1, was built in 1968 and started generating power in 1974. Nuclear power plants generally took a very long time, usually years, from construction to operation because they were so tightly regulated. TMI-1 was owned by the Metropolitan Edison Company, a utility company that provided power to 350,000 people in southern and eastern Pennsylvania. The plant was built on a narrow island in the middle of the Susquehanna River near Middletown, Pennsylvania. The second plant, called TMI-2, was where the 1979 accident would take place. It started construction in 1969 but did not receive its license to operate until 1978. A nuclear supply

Chernobyl

One of the worst nuclear power plant disasters in world history took place in 1986 at the Chernobyl plant in the former Soviet Union. Explosions at the plant blew off the reactor roof and started a fire. Huge clouds of radioactive particles were released into the atmosphere and drifted over neighboring European countries. However, Chernobyl was a type of nuclear plant that has never been built in the United States. It did not have a containment dome like those in US plants. Its operating system was difficult to control, and it was too easy to override safety systems.

company called Babcock & Wilcox manufactured the reactors for both Three Mile Island plants. They also built TMI-2's safety equipment and part of the steam supply system.

TMI-2 was capable of producing 900 megawatts of electricity. That would be enough electricity to power between 500,000 and 1 million households, depending on where they were located and how much energy they consumed. Construction took 190,000 cubic yards (152,000 cu m) of concrete, 24,000 short tons (21,600 metric tons) of steel, and 740 miles (1,184 km) of electric wiring. It cost $700 million to build. Together, TMI-1 and TMI-2 had four concrete cooling towers, the most familiar landmarks of many nuclear power plants. The towers rose 350 feet (105 m) into the sky and were used to cool the water that drove the plant's turbines. Water was cooled through the towers because

The Antinuclear Movement

As early as 1940, scientists were voicing concerns about nuclear power. In 1969, a group called the Union of Concerned Scientists formed at the Massachusetts Institute of Technology. Regular citizens also questioned the safety of nuclear energy. They formed groups such as Greenpeace to protest nuclear energy. Protests were held all over the country, especially when new plants were planned. One of the most famous groups was the Clamshell Alliance, formed in 1976 in New Hampshire to protest the construction of the Seabrook Nuclear Power Plant. The Three Mile Island accident would lead to even more protests and antinuclear activities.

returning heated water to the river would damage the environment. One of the biggest misconceptions about the Three Mile Island accident was that radioactive vapor could be released through these towers to the atmosphere, but the towers were not part of the nuclear steam supply system.

Some people protested against the plants during the planning and construction stages, and a few newspaper editorials questioned their safety. This was a time when many Americans were beginning to wonder about the safety of nuclear power plants and whether they should continue to be built. But overall, many people in the area around Three Mile Island had become accustomed to seeing the plants' cooling towers. They also knew nuclear energy was helping reduce the impact of the energy crisis by providing power that did not depend on foreign oil sources.

TMI-2 began commercial operation on December 30, 1978. Little did the utility company or the people in the surrounding area know it would operate smoothly for only three months. ⌐

*TMI-2 would operate for only three months
before the accident on March 28, 1979.*

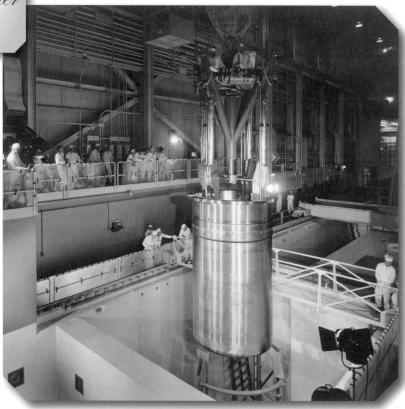

Construction of the reactor core, where fission occurs,
at the Shippingport nuclear power plant

How a Nuclear Plant Works

In order to really understand what
happened at the Three Mile Island
plant on March 28, 1979, it helps to understand
how a nuclear power plant works. It all begins with
nuclear fission, when a uranium atom splits. All

the machinery of a nuclear plant is just equipment without this nuclear reaction.

FROM ATOM TO ENERGY

The tiniest part of a nuclear reactor is an atom, which is the smallest part of an element. Every atom has a nucleus at its center, made up of protons and neutrons. Electrons also orbit around the nucleus.

A nuclear reaction is based on one simple fact: when you split a heavy atom like uranium, which is heavy because it has a high number of neutrons and protons, it releases a tremendous amount of energy. Uranium and plutonium go through a process called fission, where their atoms are split in a controlled way. Fission is created by bombarding the nucleus of an atom with neutrons, which split the atom, release more neutrons, and split more atoms, in a chain reaction. The chain reaction created by nuclear fission can release huge amounts of energy. When an atom undergoes fission, the energy

Radiation

Nuclear fission produces radiation, which is the energy and particles emitted by an unstable radioactive atom. These particles can interact with other atoms and create dangerous effects. Large doses of radiation interfere with cell growth and can cause cancer. There are four types of radiation: alpha rays, beta rays, gamma rays, and neutrons. Each affects the human body in different ways.

that once held it together is now released as heat. This is the basis of nuclear power, since that heat can be used to create electricity.

Nuclear power plants use uranium that has been processed into pellets and then sealed inside long metal tubes called fuel rods or cladding. Groups of fuel rods are then bundled together into fuel assemblies, which are used in the nuclear plant's reactor core to create heat during fission. The heat is then used to turn water into steam, which powers turbines and creates electricity.

Uranium as a fuel is much more economical than coal or oil. According to the Edison Electric Institute in its publication *Nuclear Power: Answers to Your Questions*:

> The fissioning of one atom releases 50 million times more energy than the combustion of a single carbon atom [found in] all fossil fuel. Since a single

Where Does Uranium Come From?

Nuclear power plants rely on uranium for fuel. But where does it come from? Ninety-five percent of the uranium in the United States comes from mines in New Mexico, Wyoming, Utah, Nebraska, Arizona, Texas, Washington, and Colorado. It is mined in open pits or underground mines. Then the raw uranium ore is crushed in a mill, and the uranium is extracted. This creates a powder called yellowcake (named for its rough texture and yellow color). Then it is sent to government-owned processing plants, where it is enriched and made into fuel pellets.

small reactor fuel pellet [about the size of a pencil eraser] contains trillions upon trillion of atoms, an extremely large amount of energy is released. The amount of electricity that can be generated from three small fuel pellets would require about 3.5 tons [3.2 metric tons] of coal or 12 barrels of oil to generate.[1]

CONTROLLING THE REACTION

The key to controlling the fission process is a system used inside the plant's reactor. The fuel assemblies that hold the uranium pellets have a cavity in the

Breeder Reactors

All commercial nuclear reactors throughout the world use uranium fuel to produce energy. Since World War II, though, some nuclear scientists have proposed a type of nuclear reactor, called a breeder reactor, which uses plutonium instead of uranium. In fact, a breeder reactor produces more plutonium than it uses. Some thought the excess plutonium could be used as fuel for other reactors. The idea was that it would create an inexhaustible supply of energy at a low cost, much like a continuous recycling system. Nuclear scientists who feared a possible shortage of the world's uranium supply believed breeder reactors would be advantageous compared to the traditional type of reactors.

However, experimental breeder reactor plants in the United States and other countries ultimately proved to not be practical, safe, or economical enough for regular use. Demonstration plants revealed that breeder reactors are dangerous because they use sodium for coolant, which is less stable than water. The nuclear reaction created by a breeder reactor is hard to manage and control, creating serious safety concerns. In 1963, Unit 1 at the Enrico Fermi Atomic Power Plant in Michigan became the first demonstration breeder reactor to operate in the United States. It was decommissioned in 1972 after many problems.

center for something called control rods. Like the gas pedal on a car, control rods can accelerate the fission process when they are pulled out of the fuel assembly, allowing neutrons to collide with the fuel. They then act like a brake when they are inserted into the fuel assembly and absorb the neutrons, regulating the fission process and serving as a safety feature. Plant operators regulate the rods from the control room, but in the case of a mechanical failure, the rods will automatically fall into the reactor core to slow the fission process.

Light Water Reactors

All the nuclear power plants in the United States are light water reactors, or LWRs. LWRs were designed in the 1940s and have stayed popular because they are simple in design. LWRs use uranium as a fuel and regular water as a coolant. High-pressure water passes

Fuel Rods

The way fuel rods are arranged depends on the type of reactor. A BWR usually has 4 fuel bundles of 64 rods in an 8-by-8 pattern. The cavity for the control rod is in the center. A PWR requires more fuel rods. There are usually bundles of 225 rods arranged in a 15-by-15 pattern. The control rod in the center is actually a bundle of several smaller, tube-shaped control rods. However, these arrangements can also vary, depending on the size of the power plant.

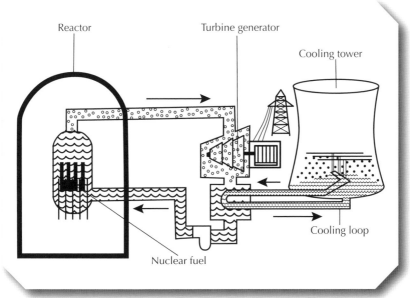

Reactor Turbine generator

Cooling tower

Cooling loop

Nuclear fuel

A boiling water reactor (BWR) pumps water in a closed cycle.

around the reactor, where it is heated, and then it moves into a steam generator.

However, there are two types of LWRs used in the United States. They differ in the way they use cooling water and the way they produce steam. One type of LWR is called a boiling water reactor (BWR). It pumps water in a closed cycle. This means the water is reused again and again and never leaves the system. The water is heated by the nuclear reaction as it moves around the fuel. When the water boils, the

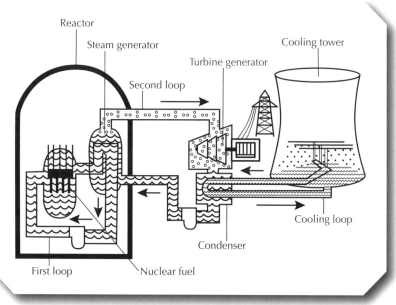

Reactor

Steam generator

Turbine generator

Cooling tower

Second loop

First loop

Nuclear fuel

Condenser

Cooling loop

Three Mile Island used a pressurized water reactor (PWR) system.

water and steam flow to the top of the reactor where they are separated. The steam is passed to the turbine generator, which it turns to create electricity. Then the steam is condensed back into water in the cooling loop and returned to the reactor.

The other type of LWR is a pressurized water reactor (PWR). This kind has two loops of coolant systems to transfer energy from the reactor to the turbine generator. The first loop pumps water through the reactor, where it is heated by the nuclear fuel, and then through a steam generator before coming around through the reactor again. A second loop of water pumps through the other side of the steam generator, which creates the steam that goes to the turbine generator. The steam generator basically exchanges the heat from the first loop of water to the second loop. The steam in the second loop condenses into water and pumps back through the steam generator in a continuous cycle.

In the PWR system, the water used for steam must be cooled before it is sent back to the reactor for reuse. Cool circulating water—which usually comes from a nearby lake, ocean, or river—is piped through a condenser, where it absorbs the heat and condenses the steam back to water. The cooling water is now hot and cannot yet be returned to its source. It is then piped to a cooling tower, where its temperature lowers. These

Nuclear Waste

One problem common to all nuclear plants is disposing of radioactive waste. The biggest challenge is disposing spent, or used, fuel rods that can no longer create fission. These are removed from the reactor during the refueling process and placed in a concrete spent fuel pool. Most fuel needs to remain in a pool for 10 to 20 years before it can be moved to permanent storage. But due to the high volume of spent fuel, many plants are running out of room in spent fuel pools. The NRC estimates that US spent fuel pools will be full by 2015. The government is attempting to construct new long-term storage facilities for nuclear waste.

are the large, concrete towers most people associate with nuclear plants.

TMI-1 and TMI-2 were both PWRs. The accident at TMI-2 began with a malfunction in a pump that fed water to the steam generator. It was the first of several events to disrupt the normal operation of the PWR system. ⌒

The cooling towers are the most recognizable landmarks
at the Three Mile Island nuclear power plant.

*The containment building, which houses the reactor,
was the scene of the plant emergency at Three Mile Island.*

EMERGENCY

he first few minutes and hours after the initial accident at TMI-2 were confusing. Lights and alarms continued flashing and wailing in the control room. If all the systems in the plant had been working as they were designed, they would have already brought the incident under control. The backup coolant pumps had kicked on automatically. They were trying to send cooling water into the feedwater system. But because valves had been left closed for maintenance, the water had nowhere to go. The valves should never have been closed while the reactor was operating. This was a violation of one of the NRC's most important rules. As an NRC source later stated,

> If you take all of these pumps out at once, even for a limited time, you're supposed to hit the down button and shut the reactor down in a . . . hurry.[1]

Harold Denton, the NRC chief of reactor operations, later said in a press briefing, "There would have been an entirely different outcome if they (the pumps) had been operational, as they should have been."[2] With the fresh cold water unable to enter the cooling system, the steam generator began to boil dry. The temperatures inside the reactor were climbing.

HUMAN ERROR

Despite the closed valves, other systems of the plant were still operating properly. Only two minutes into the accident, the high-pressure injection pumps automatically came on to feed more water into the cooling system. However, it was at this point that the plant operators made an error in judgment. They had been receiving conflicting signals and information about what was actually going on in the cooling system. They thought there was more water in the cooling system than there actually was. They were concerned, then, that too much water would replace the necessary cushion of steam in the pressurizer system. So after only four minutes, the shift

The Control Room

The heart of a nuclear power plant is its reactor, which produces the energy. But the brain of the plant is its control room. Here the operators sit and monitor huge banks of switches, monitors, lights, and alarms to run the plant. They can monitor the function of the plant and see when a potential malfunction or problem arises. The control room is constantly staffed 24 hours a day by at least three people. At the time of the accident, TMI-2 had six people on duty. A control room even has its own separate air supply, restrooms, and heating and cooling systems, and it is also protected from radiation. In the event of an emergency, this allows the operators to continue running the plant without ever leaving the control room.

Control room personnel go through extensive training before they can perform their jobs. First they attend classroom training, and then they learn on a simulator. A simulator is a full-size replica of a real control room, with lights and switches connected to a computer. This way, operators can respond to simulated emergency situations before they actually begin working at a real nuclear plant. Operators must also be licensed by the NRC to prove they have been trained, and they must continue training throughout their careers.

supervisor ordered one of the injection pumps to be shut down and the others reduced in power. The operators also decided to shut off the four reactor coolant pumps, huge pieces of equipment each the size of a small truck. As J. Samuel Walker describes in his book *Three Mile Island*,

> *A little more than an hour into the accident the pumps began to shake so furiously that the operators could feel the vibrations in the control room. This was a result of the rising heat in the core and the growing presence of steam in the coolant. The operators still did not recognize that they were dealing with a loss-of-coolant accident, and in accordance with their training . . . they shut down two of the pumps to prevent damage to them.*[3]

As a result of these actions, the reactor was no longer receiving enough cooling water. The water level in the core dropped until water was no longer covering all the fuel rods. The fuel rods began overheating. The zirconium cladding ruptured on the long metal tubes that held the fuel pellets, and the pellets began melting. It would not be discovered until months after the accident that approximately one-half of the reactor core melted at this stage. These later investigations revealed that the temperature in the core had probably reached 4,000 degrees Fahrenheit (2,204°C) or even higher.

The upper sections of the core slumped, meaning they crumbled into a molten pile. Radioactive gases usually contained inside the fuel rods escaped into the coolant system. Then they made their way into the reactor building through the regulating valve that was still stuck open. Radioactive water was still being pumped into the overflow tanks and spilling out on to the floor of the auxiliary building. The auxiliary building's ventilation system was releasing the radioactivity from the water into the environment. Alarms began sounding to indicate high levels of radiation in different parts of the plant. Around 7:20 a.m., the emergency at TMI had been elevated to a general site emergency because of the levels of radiation inside the reactor containment building.

What began as an incident that could have been prevented in the first seven or eight minutes was now a full-fledged emergency.

Warning Signs?

Before the Three Mile Island accident, relief valves in other nuclear reactors designed by Babcock & Wilcox had stuck open at least nine times, just as one stuck open in TMI-2. The company had not informed its other nuclear plants about the failures, however. They did not upgrade their training programs, either. So the TMI-2 operators had no way of knowing this kind of malfunction could occur and create a loss of coolant in the reactor.

Workers at Three Mile Island are checked for exposure to radioactivity after a general site emergency is called the day of the accident.

Spreading the News

By 7:00 a.m., a team had assembled at TMI-2 to help the operators. They notified the Pennsylvania Emergency Management Agency, the Pennsylvania Bureau of Radiation Protection, and the US Department of Energy's Radiological Assistance Program. By 8:00 a.m., the NRC was notified. The operators had already determined the nuclear fuel had been damaged. Immediately, teams of technicians went out to check radiation levels in surrounding areas. Even though radiation had been released from the reactor into the auxiliary building and then into the environment, the technicians found radiation levels in surrounding areas to be either very low or undetectable. By 9:00 a.m., the plant operators had discovered the radioactive water pumping into the auxiliary building. They shut down the pump, which slowed the release of radiation through the ventilation system. The operators also began pumping water back into the cooling system to cool the core.

News of the accident reached the public through a radio broadcast at 8:25 a.m. Soon, reporters from newspapers and networks all over the world began arriving at Three Mile Island. Lieutenant Governor William Scranton held a press conference to explain the TMI situation. Right from the start of the accident, Metropolitan Edison and the governor's office had problems exchanging accurate information. For this reason, the lieutenant governor made statements later proven false. At first, he simply stated that, according to Met-Ed, "there is and was no danger to public health and safety" and although there was "a small release of radiation to the environment . . . no increase in normal radiation levels has been detected."[4] However, later events would show that the information the lieutenant governor received from Met-Ed was inaccurate.

At 4:30 p.m. the lieutenant governor gave another press conference:

"We've Got a Problem"

Mike Pintek, news director at the radio station that first reported the accident, called the plant for more information. He was connected right to the control room. A man there told him, "I can't talk now, we've got a problem." When Pintek called the Met-Ed headquarters, he was told, "There was a problem with a feedwater pump. The plant is shut down. We're working on it. There's no danger off-site. No danger to the general public." Pintek later said, "And that is the story we went with at 8:25. I tried to tone it down so people wouldn't be alarmed."[5]

This is an update on the incident at Three-Mile Island Nuclear Power Plant today. This situation is more complex than the company first led us to believe. We are taking more tests. And at this point, we believe there is still no danger to public health. Metropolitan Edison has given you and us conflicting information. We just concluded a meeting with company officials and hope this briefing will clear up most of your questions. There has been a release of radioactivity into the environment. The magnitude of this release is still being determined, but there is no evidence yet that it has resulted in the presence of dangerous levels. The company has informed us that from about 11 a.m. until about 1:30 p.m., Three-Mile Island discharged into the air, steam that contained detectable amounts of radiation.[6]

Emergency Siren

Two days after the initial accident and at the height of the crisis, the eerie wail of the town's emergency siren suddenly sounded through Harrisburg, more than ten miles (16 km) away from the plant. No one, not even officials, knew who had set off the siren, but it added to everyone's fears of a catastrophe taking place at the plant. "That siren was like a knife in my chest," Governor Richard Thornburgh remembers thinking. "I thought, 'What on Earth? Where did that come from?'"[7]

By 8:00 p.m., the reactor system had cooled enough that the coolant pumps could be turned back on. Now the process of removing all that extra heat from the reactor could begin. Officials were also beginning to investigate just how extensive the damage to the reactor had been. Even though the threat of a total reactor meltdown seemed to have passed, the public was beginning to hear more and more news about the crisis, and they were beginning to worry.

Workers measure radiation levels at the Three Mile Island visitor center across from the plant.

*TV newscaster Walter Cronkite informs the nation of
the Three Mile Island accident.*

MARCH 29, 1979

On the evening of March 28, 1979,
journalist Walter Cronkite said on the
CBS Evening News:

> It was the first step in a nuclear nightmare; as far as we
> know at this hour, no worse than that. But a government

official said that a breakdown in an atomic power plant in Pennsylvania today is probably the worst nuclear accident to date.[1]

Thursday, March 29, dawned with widespread national media coverage of the Three Mile Island accident. Met-Ed executives appeared on television shows such as ABC's *Good Morning America* and NBC's *The Today Show*. They admitted that small amounts of radiation had leaked from the plant, but said it was under control and no one in the surrounding area was in danger.

ALERT AND INFORMED

Throughout the morning of March 29, it seemed as if the situation at Three Mile Island would soon be under control. The reactor had not yet cooled to safe levels, but overall, the situation was improving. The plant seemed to be stable, and operators felt they would soon be able to shut it down safely. Radiation monitoring continued in the area, but no abnormally high levels had been noted in the air. The US Food and Drug Administration was beginning to test food, milk, and water in the surrounding area to make sure none of it had been contaminated with radiation. William Dornsife, a nuclear engineer for the state of Pennsylvania, said the emergency was "essentially over."[2]

However, many officials and politicians were beginning to ask questions about the accident, such as why it had taken place and what dangers might still be ahead for people in the area. During the day, several congressional representatives from the area visited the plant and spoke to plant and NRC officials. Governor Thornburgh was still concerned about severe

The China Syndrome

As the Three Mile Island accident was taking place, a movie called *The China Syndrome* was playing in many area theaters. It took its name from the hypothesis that if a nuclear reactor went out of control and got too hot, it could melt through the Earth's crust, into the core of the planet, and continue "all the way to China." The name was based on the popular misconception that China was directly "under," or opposite, the United States. As early as the 1960s, scientists were already thinking about this possibility. They asked the nuclear industry in the United States and around the world to develop safeguards to keep the China Syndrome from ever taking place.

The China Syndrome movie was loosely based on a real incident that took place at the Rancho Seco Nuclear Power Plant in California. However, in the movie and during the actual incident itself, the China Syndrome did not actually take place. In real life and in the movie, the plant shut down exactly as designed. Ironically, the partial meltdown of the reactor at Three Mile Island mirrored some of the movie's events, but again, the hypothesized catastrophe never occurred. It did not escape the notice of the media, however, that the movie was playing at the time of the TMI incident.

damage to the reactor core and how that would affect the public. He was still mulling over the possibility of evacuations. So on March 29, Lieutenant Governor Scranton and two aides decided to tour TMI-2. Scranton's experience is recounted in the PBS documentary *Meltdown at Three Mile Island*:

> "It occurred to me, 'Someone's got to go down there and look at that place . . .' and being 30 years old, and maybe thinking I was more immortal than I really was, I said, 'I'm going to go down there,'" he later recounted. Scranton revealed a sense of foreboding as he arrived at the plant, ". . . You just drive up and there they are. They're magnificently huge, beautifully engineered symbols of the power of technological society to do good and the power of technological society to do harm."[3]

Met-Ed would only allow one person to enter the auxiliary

Dosimeters

How do workers and visitors to nuclear power plants keep track of how much radiation they receive? They wear a device called a dosimeter, which measures the amount of radiation (such as gamma and beta rays) their bodies are exposed to. Because radiation cannot be felt or seen, a dosimeter keeps track of how much radiation a body absorbs and when it has reached a dangerous level.

building, where radioactive water was
still pooling on the floor. Scranton
put on protective clothing—plastic
suit, rubber boots, and a respirator—
and toured the building. He reported
that the plant's employees seemed to
be dealing calmly with the problems.

Later in the day, Governor
Thornburgh held his first press
conference since the accident. He
assured the public that "there is no
cause for alarm, nor any reason to
disrupt your daily routine, nor any
reason to feel that public health has
been affected by the events on Three
Mile Island." But he also added, "It
is very important that all of us remain
alert and informed."[4]

MISCOMMUNICATIONS

Despite the governor's reassuring
words, everything was not back
to normal at TMI-2 and in the
surrounding area. That afternoon,
a helicopter flying above the plant

Preparing for the Worst

As the crisis at the plant
unfolded, Mayor Ken
Meyers of Goldsboro
talked to his city council
about the possible effects
of radiation from the
plant: "We told them also
of our evacuation plans in
case the Governor would
declare an emergency and
that we would all have to
leave. Of course, right
away they gave us ques-
tions: 'Well, what should
we do? Do you think it's
safe that we should stay
or do you think we should
go?' The ones that I talked
to, I told them: 'Use your
own judgment. We dare
not tell you to leave your
homes.'"[5]

*Governor Richard Thornburgh, left, and Lieutenant Governor William
Scranton, right, at a press conference following the accident*

detected a brief, heavy burst of radiation from the
vent. The plant reported it to the NRC, which was
not concerned by it.

That afternoon there was another release—this
time of radioactive water. It was at a level well below
NRC guidelines, meaning the radiation level was
low enough not to cause a health risk. This was the
slightly contaminated wastewater from the plant's
toilets, drains, showers, and laundry facilities.

This water, which usually contained little, if any, radiation, was routinely diluted and then discharged into the Susquehanna River. On Wednesday, the day of the accident, Met-Ed had told the plant not to release this water as a safety precaution. But by Thursday afternoon, 400,000 gallons (1,520,000 L) of this water had accumulated in a holding tank, and it was close to overflowing. It was slightly contaminated with xenon gas, but still well under the limits for normal release into the environment.

However, what should have been a routine release turned into a misunderstanding. As the plant began releasing water, NRC Chairman Joseph Hendrie was upset, believing Met-Ed had taken this action without consulting the NRC. He was concerned about how people would feel if they knew Met-Ed was dumping water into the river one day after the accident. Confusion

From Grass to Cows to Milk

In the area surrounding any nuclear power plant, technicians routinely test milk from dairy cows. A release of radiation into the environment would contaminate grass. Cows that ate the grass would become contaminated, and radiation would also pass into their milk, where it could then be consumed by humans. Dairy farmers whose farms are near a nuclear plant are paid to provide a monthly sample of their cows' milk to the power plant's technicians.

and lack of communication forced Met-Ed to stop the discharge after releasing only 40,000 gallons (152,000 L). Eventually, the NRC and Met-Ed straightened out the misunderstanding, and the release resumed. But the situation had revealed growing tension between the NRC, the state, and TMI owners.

WARNING SIGNS

As it turned out, the overall feeling that the situation at TMI-2 was resolving was premature. Officials still did not realize part of the plant's reactor core had actually been uncovered and the core had suffered a partial meltdown. As stated in the presidential commission report:

> At 6:30 p.m. [on March 29th], . . . James Higgins, an NRC reactor inspector, received the results of an analysis of the reactor's coolant water. It showed that core damage was far more substantial

"Just Something You Live With"

Many people who lived in the area surrounding Three Mile Island were concerned about what was taking place during the accident, but they did not panic. A woman who lived in nearby Golds-boro said about the plant, "It's just something you live with, but this makes you think a little bit." She added, "My husband and I built this house our-selves, so it would take a lot to make us leave."[6]

*than . . . anticipated. At 10:00 p.m., Higgins telephoned
the Governor's office with the new information and indicated
that a greater possibility of radiation releases existed. Nothing
had changed inside the plant, only NRC's awareness of the
seriousness of the damage.*[7]

Officials had initially estimated that only
approximately 1 percent of the fuel rods had been
damaged, but many months later, they would
eventually learn that closer to 50 percent had actually
been damaged. This meant that during the accident,
the potential for the release of radiation was much
greater than officials had thought. As Thursday,
March 29, became Friday, March 30, the events
at Three Mile Island, which so many people had
thought were under control, blossomed into a crisis.

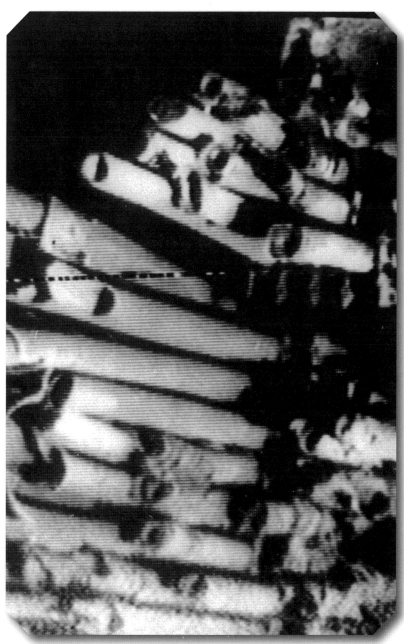

With the help of a video camera, TMI technicians later discovered the
alarming number of broken fuel rods at the bottom of the reactor.

*Officials were concerned when radioactive material was vented
from the plant into the atmosphere.*

March 30, 1979

ust before 8:00 a.m. on Friday, March 30,
TMI workers had to release pressure from
a tank inside the plant's auxiliary building. This tank
had been accumulating radioactive gas produced by
the damage to the reactor core. Workers had been

carefully "burping" this gas into the atmosphere in amounts too small to be dangerous. But when the gas levels in the holding tank became too high and began putting pressure on the cooling system, workers opened a vent valve. This would vent more radioactive gas into the atmosphere than before, but it would also lower the pressure and prevent a more drastic event.

However, the operators in the control room began this process without consulting Met-Ed or informing the state and the NRC because they did not expect radiation levels to rise too sharply. Workers in the company helicopter monitored radiation levels above the cooling stacks as the gases began venting. The workers recorded a reading of 1,200 millirems per hour at approximately 130 feet (39 m) above the stack. This was well above normal readings, and it would escalate the crisis at the plant.

Evacuation!

What happened next was the result of miscommunication between the plant, the NRC, and local and state authorities. The radiation had been recorded many feet above the ground, which meant that the people below would never be exposed to those levels. In reality, the reading on the ground was only 14 millirems. However, when news of the high radiation reading made its way to the NRC, the reports mistakenly indicated that the level had been recorded near the ground. Based on this misunderstood data, the NRC and the state became involved. At 12:30 p.m., Governor Thornburgh called a press conference and announced:

Based on advice of the Chairman of the Nuclear Regulatory Commission and in the interest of taking every precaution,

Rem and Millirem

When radioactivity was first discovered in the early twentieth century, a roentgen was the unit of measurement for the amount of radioactivity from substances such as uranium. It was named for Wilhelm Röntgen, the scientist who discovered X-rays, which are radioactive rays similar to gamma rays. Eventually, scientists learned just how harmful different types of radioactivity could be to the human body, and they developed more specific forms of measurement.

At the time of the Three Mile Island accident, the unit used to measure the amount of radioactivity was a rem. A rem (which stands for "roentgen equivalent man") measures the actual dose of radiation a human body absorbs. Adult workers in a nuclear power plant are supposed to receive no more than 5 rem per year, but the body will not start to show effects of even the lowest level of radiation sickness until it has received a dose of at least 150 rem in a very short amount of time. A millirem is one-thousandth of a rem. It is used to calculate the very small doses of radiation most people encounter in their daily lives, such as from natural background radiation, medical procedures such as X-rays, and the natural radiation found in food. The average American receives a dose of 620 millirem, or 0.62 rem, every year.

I am advising those who may be particularly susceptible to the effects of radiation, that is, pregnant women and preschool age children, to leave the area within a five-mile [8-km] radius of the Three Mile Island facility until further notice.[1]

In addition to this advisory, all other people within a ten-mile (16-km) radius of the plant were told to stay inside their homes.

But the NRC's recommendation and the governor's announcement did not take into account just how difficult it would be to evacuate so many people quickly. Like all nuclear plants, TMI had an evacuation plan (which is required before a plant can be licensed for operation), but that did not mean local and state authorities were ready to put an actual evacuation into effect. Denton commented, "I did not give any weight to whatever hardship

Deciding to Go

Although the evacuation advisory was only for pregnant women and young children, Middletown resident Robin Stuart recalled how all residents still had to make a decision about whether to leave town or stay put: "My father wouldn't leave. . . . Dad was thinking of his neighbors and his neighborhood and thinking about the possibility of looting and he was going to stand guard . . . He was one of the heroes to me because he felt that sense of duty."[2]

As empty streets show, pregnant women and young children were not the only ones who evacuated the communities near the Three Mile Island plant.

evacuation might cause. I saw the key issue as being one of timeliness, to move rapidly."[3]

As a result of Thornburgh's press conference, people in the Harrisburg area began making plans to leave their homes quickly. Phone lines were jammed as relatives tried contacting each other, long lines formed at gas stations, and traffic gridlock developed. Parents pulled their children out of school or rushed home to wait for them. People were confused, concerned, and angry.

Despite the governor's
instructions, more than just pregnant
women and young children began
evacuating. According to J. Samuel
Walker in his book *Three Mile Island*:

> An estimated 83 percent of pregnant
> women and preschool children within
> a five-mile [8-km] radius, or
> approximately 3,500 individuals,
> evacuated. They were joined by many
> of their neighbors. Approximately
> 144,000 people within a fifteen-mile
> [24-km] radius of the plant evacuated
> at some point during the crisis, and
> 51 percent of them did so on Friday.
> The streets of Goldsboro were deserted.[4]

Most of the people who left
their homes went to stay with family
members or friends outside the
immediate area of TMI. Some
fled much farther, to relatives
in other parts of the country.
Evacuation centers set up by civil
defense authorities received only a

Looking for a Story

During the evacuation, the news media was looking for dramatic footage of people fleeing their homes. But when they arrived in Middletown, they found only empty streets. When a pickup truck loaded with household goods suddenly appeared, reporters swarmed around it. They discovered that it was not a terrified family leaving the area, but simply someone new moving into the community.

small percentage of the evacuees.
The Hershey Sports Arena, which
was prepared to handle as many
as 14,000 people, never housed
or fed more than 180 people.
Despite residents' fear and anger
about evacuating, many officials
stressed how generally composed the
population was. They evacuated in an
orderly fashion without panic.

THE WHITE HOUSE GETS INVOLVED

On Friday, the White House
finally joined the unfolding
crisis at Three Mile Island. That
morning, President Jimmy Carter
was informed of the unusually high
radiation reading from TMI that was
mistakenly assumed to be ground-
level data. President Carter had
been in the US Navy and served in
the nuclear submarine program, so
he was familiar with the hazards of
radiation and how it could threaten
public health. While in the navy,

A Welcome Distraction

People who took shelter
in the Hershey Sports
Arena were overwhelmed
by reporters looking for
stories. One pregnant
woman became so dizzy
from camera flashbulbs,
officials were afraid she
was going into labor.
The Hershey Company
decided to provide some
relief for these evacuees.
They offered free tours
of their zoo, amusement
park, and Chocolate
World Attraction, none of
which was open for the
season.

Carter had even participated in the cleanup of an experimental nuclear reactor in Canada that had suffered a serious accident in 1952. However, President Carter was not an enthusiastic supporter of nuclear energy and considered it a "last resort" energy source.

Carter was briefed on the situation at TMI and told there were some communication issues between the plant, state officials, and the NRC. Not knowing the NRC had recommended an evacuation just a short time before, he said about evacuating that "I think it would be good to err on the side of safety."[5] President Carter also decided to send Denton to TMI as his personal representative at the site. From then on, Denton would evaluate the situation at TMI and advise the president.

But even as the evacuation was announced and people began moving

Watch the Town

Robert Reid, the mayor of Middletown, was frustrated with the lack of accurate information about the TMI crisis. His town had no real evacuation plan in place. He later said, "People left their jobs, came home, packed their cars and their children. And I remember standing on the corner and cars zipping past me and people hollering out the window, 'Watch the town.' . . . Things were starting to get a little hectic."[6] Not only did he have to help citizens of his city evacuate calmly, but he also had to guard against anyone, such as looters, taking advantage of the situation.

out of the TMI area, a new problem was developing
that would escalate the actual crisis. The confusing
and conflicting information surrounding this
problem would reveal just how difficult it was to
know what was really happening at Three Mile Island
and how dangerous it was.

*Harold Denton of the Nuclear Regulatory Commission became
President Carter's personal representative regarding Three Mile Island.*

Any attempts to cool the core were thwarted by a hydrogen bubble occupying the top of the reactor pressure vessel, shown here from the outside.

THE HYDROGEN BUBBLE

s the events of Thursday and Friday unfolded, it was apparent to both Met-Ed and the NRC that there had been more damage to the reactor core than they previously thought. For that reason, they knew cooling the core and

safely shutting down the plant was going to be more
complicated than expected. But the core was not
cooling as quickly as it should. One of the reasons
why was the presence of a hydrogen gas bubble at
the top of the pressure vessel, the container that
housed the core. Officials first detected this bubble
at 11:30 a.m. on Friday. The bubble was a major
obstacle in trying to cool the reactor core.

THE BUBBLE

Severe damage to the plant's fuel
rods had produced the hydrogen
bubble. It took up approximately
1,000 cubic feet (30 cu m) inside
the pressure vessel, occupying most
of the available space inside it. This
hindered any efforts to cool the
core. The operators needed to inject
coolant from the emergency cooling
system into the core, but they first
needed to lower the pressure inside
the vessel. But that might have made
the hydrogen bubble grow even
bigger, which in turn could have
meant even less coolant reaching the

Hydrogen Explosions

In March 2011, the
world learned just how
dangerous hydrogen
explosions can be.
After being devastated
by an earthquake and
tsunami, Japan's Fuku-
shima Daiichi nuclear
plant experienced three
hydrogen explosions after
workers were unable
to cool three reactors.
These explosions injured
workers and damaged
buildings, but the reactor
vessels remained intact.

core. There was also the fear that if enough oxygen mixed with the hydrogen bubble, then the smallest spark could make it explode and cause a complete core meltdown.

At a news conference on Saturday, March 31, NRC Chairman Joseph Hendrie told the crowd of reporters, "The principal problem we have right now is to work out a means of dealing with that gas bubble. We have to get that gas bubble out of the reactor."[1] The NRC wanted help finding solutions to deal with the hydrogen bubble, so they contacted the Idaho National Engineering Laboratory and defense contractor company EG&G in Idaho Falls. They had a workforce of 4,000 nuclear technicians. EG&G actually constructed a model of TMI to help them find a solution.

Four Possible Plans

Nuclear engineers came up with four possible methods to deal with the bubble. They were all risky to one degree or another. The first plan was to increase the pressure inside the vessel and collapse the bubble. Then it would dissolve in the coolant water that was flooding the core and be pumped away into the plant's wastewater tanks. Another plan was to decrease the pressure inside the vessel, which could be risky in the long run. If it caused the bubble to expand, it would displace the cooling water and expose even more of the reactor core.

The other two plans were the riskiest. One involved sinking the bubble by dropping the water level, exposing the core, and then flooding the reactor with freshwater. The other plan was to restart the reactor and create so much heat that the cooling water would turn into steam and break the bubble. But this plan was the riskiest of all, since engineers believed they might not be able to start or control the reactor because so many fuel rods were broken or damaged. A damaged rod could also scrape on something and create a spark, igniting the bubble.

With so little known about the hydrogen bubble, officials discussed the possibility of evacuating even more people. If an explosion took place and the core melted down, the release of radiation into the environment would be severe. Officials began

The Bubble Buster

After so much stress and uncertainly, there were a few moments of humor once things began quieting down in Middletown. The restaurant at the Elks Lodge social club renamed their cheeseburger "The Meltdown." A bowl of chili with beans became the "Bubble Buster."

A potential evacuation due to the threat of the hydrogen bubble would have affected a large area and a large number of people.

planning for the evacuation of a 20-mile (32-km) ring around the plant, which included more than 600,000 people.

CONFLICTING THEORIES

Experts from all over the country disagreed if there was an immediate threat of the hydrogen bubble exploding. Some felt it would take eight to ten days before the bubble would reach the point of exploding, and in that time, nuclear engineers could shrink it so it would no longer be a threat. Denton and his group were among those who believed there was no immediate possibility of an explosion taking place.

But others worried it could explode at any moment. After talking with nuclear physicists around the country, Roger Mattson, a director at the Office of Nuclear Reactor Regulation, believed the bubble could explode at any second. Mattson was angry an evacuation was not already in progress. "I'm not sure why you are not moving people," he declared. "I don't know what we are protecting at this point. I think we

A Personal Reaction

Lieutenant Governor Scranton discussed his reaction to the hydrogen bubble threat: "I was quite unnerved. When I heard . . . people whom we trusted and thought knew what they were talking about were speculating at the possibility of a hydrogen bubble, I, for the first time, got frightened. I will readily admit it. . . . It was frightening to me as a husband of a pregnant woman. It was frightening to me as a public official because this was the first time anybody with a really good head on their shoulders was saying this could happen."[2]

ought to be moving people."[3] The debate between these two groups of scientists leaked to the media and actually increased the public's fear. People began to fear an explosion they were told would be the equivalent of a hydrogen bomb going off in their neighborhood.

But the crisis over the hydrogen bubble seemed to shrink almost as quickly as it appeared. First came the news that the temperature inside the reactor was dropping. By Sunday, April 1, the hydrogen bubble fear turned

---

Rising Fears

On Saturday, March 31, the Associated Press released an alarming news story to its wire services, which then distributed it to newspapers and television stations all over the country:

HARRISBURG, Pa. (AP) – Federal officials said Saturday night that the gas bubble inside the crippled nuclear reactor at Three Mile Island is showing signs of becoming potentially explosive, complicating decisions on whether to mount risky operation to remove the gas.

Officials said earlier that tens of thousands of people might have to be evacuated if engineers decided to try to remove the bubble, operations that could risk a meltdown of the reactor and the release of highly radioactive material into the atmosphere.

But the Nuclear Regulatory Commission said Saturday night that it might be equally risky not to try the operations, because the bubble showed signs of gradually turning into a potentially explosive mixture that could wreck the already damaged reactor.[4]

With details of a possible explosion and potential evacuations, the news release frightened the public. The release and miscommunication was one reason why President Carter decided to visit Three Mile Island himself.

out to have been a false alarm. The two teams of scientists finally agreed there was no oxygen present in the pressure vessel. Without oxygen, there was no threat of explosion. And by the end of the day, Met-Ed had successfully reduced the size of the bubble drastically. According to the *Washington Post*:

> What did happen was a gradual bleeding off of the hydrogen that had formed on the top of the reactor. It was a delicate balancing act in which engineers and specialists experimented with varying pressures . . . inside the reactor's primary coolant system.
>
> The coolant then carried the hydrogen in the form of small bubbles to the pressurizer, a cylindrical dome that rose slightly higher than the reactor. Nozzles inside the pressurizer sprayed the hydrogen-laden coolant into the top of the pressurizer where it gave off the hydrogen like fizz from a soda pop.

Lead Bricks

As the plant operators reduced the bubble's size, there was one problem with the recombiner devices that would turn the hydrogen and oxygen back into water: their controls were located in the auxiliary building, where there were high levels of radioactive contamination. Met-Ed used lead to shield the operators from radiation as they used the controls. Tons of lead bricks from all over the country arrived on flatbed trucks and in cargo planes. The bricks were cemented into a huge igloo shape over the recombiner controls to protect the operators.

A vent in the top of the pressurizer allowed the hydrogen, which was radioactive, to escape into the containment building.

In the containment building, hydrogen and oxygen were converted back into water by devices called recombiners.[5]

As fears about the hydrogen bubble slowly went away, people began to feel that perhaps the worst was over. Some returned to their homes. For many people, one simple event relieved any lingering fears: President Carter's visit to Three Mile Island.

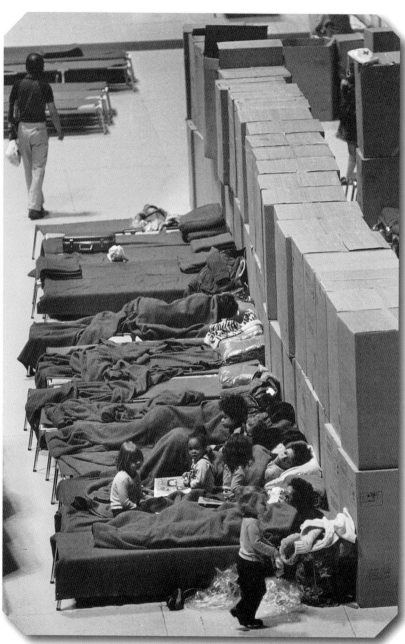

As fears of the hydrogen bubble calmed, those residents who had
evacuated began making plans for returning to their homes.

During his visit to TMI, President Carter, third from left, speaks with the Denton, left, and Governor Thornburgh, second from left.

THE CRISIS RESOLVED

Any fears the public may still have had about TMI, the hydrogen bubble, and the possibility of a meltdown were considerably diminished when President Carter arrived on Sunday, April 1. The idea to have the president tour the accident site came from one of his own cabinet members, who felt it would be the best way to calm the public's fears and show the president's concern. Carter's background also made him well suited for the trip:

> Carter was personally very concerned about the problem at the nuclear plant and he was surely better equipped than any previous president or any political figure to take a leadership role for the crisis. He had campaigned for the presidency by telling people he was a nuclear physicist and nuclear engineer. And he had written in his autobiography, "Why Not The Best?," about his role with an early Navy crisis team that had helped disassemble a damaged reactor core at a plant in Canada.[1]

Carter also felt the media had unnecessarily exaggerated the dangers at TMI and alarmed the public. As he had watched network news coverage of the events at TMI, Carter commented,

> There are too many people talking. And my impression is that half of them don't know what they are talking about. . . . Get those people to speak with one voice.[2]

With this in mind, Carter decided to make the visit to Three Mile Island. His staff asked Denton if they thought a presidential visit would help the situation. "Yes," Denton replied. "I think it would be a great help."[3]

A PRESIDENTIAL VISIT

President Carter and his wife, Rosalynn, traveled by helicopter to an air force base in Middletown, where Governor Thornburgh and several NRC officials met them. The chief of the Air National Guard Fire Department, Charles Kline, told a reporter that Carter's visit "has helped morale tremendously up here—they think if it's safe for the president of the United States to come up, it's not too bad."[4]

The president's group traveled to TMI by motorcade. When they arrived at the plant, they put yellow booties over their shoes so they would not track any ground contamination out of the plant area. They were also given dosimeters. Carter spent a little more than a half hour touring the plant and visiting the control room. Officials and plant operators

A Shot in the Arm

Middletown Mayor Robert Reid later said President Carter's visit really helped boost the morale of everyone in his city: "People weren't talking to one another. They were cooped up in their homes, and when he came, it seemed like everyone came out to see the president and it was really a shot in the arm."[5]

briefed him on the current situation.
Then Carter traveled along streets
lined with cheering people to a news
conference in Middletown. After
his two-minute speech, he left the
area. Some local people were not
impressed by the president's visit, but
others felt reassured. A 16-year-old
boy named Fred Lynch said, "The
president of the United States doesn't
just walk into a danger area. It kind of
makes you feel comfortable."[6]

A Sigh of Relief

The president's visit marked a
turning point in the TMI crisis.
Later that same day, officials
determined the hydrogen bubble was
no longer in danger of exploding.
Despite the positive turn of events,
however, the NRC still wanted to be
cautious. They discussed what they
would say at a press conference on
Monday, April 2:

Just in Case

Even the president's visit
on Sunday did not reas-
sure everyone around
TMI. During Mass, Catho-
lic priests granted their
parishioners general
absolution, something
usually done only dur-
ing war or other times
when people are endan-
gered and may not be
able to return to church
again. Area hospitals
also discharged patients
who did not need critical
care, making room for a
potential influx of people
with radiation poisoning.
These "just in case" mea-
sures showed that people
still did not feel confident.

We wanted to go slow on saying it was good news. We wanted to say it is good news, do not panic, we think we have got it under control, things look better, but we did not want to firmly and finally conclude that there was no problem. We had to save some wiggle room in order to preserve credibility. That was our judgment.[7]

Slowly, people who had evacuated the area began returning to their homes. On April 4, schools outside the five-mile (8-km) radius of TMI reopened, although the advisory for young children and pregnant women remained in effect

---

Potassium Iodide

One of the precautions taken during the TMI crisis was to stockpile a large amount of potassium iodide. Radioactive iodine-131 may have been released into the atmosphere if there had been an explosion or meltdown. It could have settled onto grass where cows grazed, and then humans could have ingested it through milk or other animal products. Iodine-131 lodges in the human thyroid gland and can cause cancer and other health problems. However, if an affected person takes potassium iodide in the right amount at the right time, it can block iodine-131 from the thyroid.

On Friday afternoon, March 30, the White House instructed the Food and Drug Administration to ensure there were enough doses of potassium iodide for the population surrounding TMI in case of a release of radiation. Over the next five days, more than 225,000 doses of potassium iodide arrived in Harrisburg, where they were stored in a warehouse. With the threat of the hydrogen bubble still worrying officials, they considered distributing doses to anyone living within a 30-minute warning time of the plant. However, Governor Thornburgh ultimately decided not to distribute the drug. He was worried it would confuse people and lead to a panic. Later, the doses were moved to a warehouse in Arkansas.

for a few more days. But by Friday, April 6, the Office of Civil Defense estimated that 90 percent of those who had left the area had returned. On April 9, 1979, the crisis was officially declared over.

THE INVESTIGATIONS BEGIN

The crisis may have been over, but the questions about what had taken place at Three Mile Island were just beginning. In a speech on April 5, President Carter announced he was creating an independent commission to investigate the causes of the TMI accident as well as address how nuclear safety could be improved. The President's Commission on the Accident at Three Mile Island was formed on April 11. There were 12 people on the commission, and the White House deliberately avoided anyone with very strong views for or against nuclear power. They wanted the members to be open-minded and

Lasting Effects

Even as the hydrogen bubble shrank and things looked better for TMI, mental health officials worried about long-term effects on people in the area. Bob Davis, who worked for a local mental health clinic, said, "When this dies down, I think it will hit us. A lot of people will want to talk about what they went through, that they felt inadequate in the crisis and embarrassment at being scared."[8]

As most people returned to their homes, the evacuation advisory for pregnant women and young children remained in effect for a few additional days.

objective. The commission had only six months to examine the events at TMI and write a report. On October 30, 1979, they presented more than 2,200 pages of explanations and reports about the incident. The commission said,

To prevent nuclear accidents as serious as Three Mile Island, fundamental changes will be necessary in the organization, procedures, and practices—and above all—in the attitudes of the Nuclear Regulatory Commission and, to the extent that the institutions we investigated are typical, of the nuclear industry.[9]

The commission also stressed that many of the mistakes during the TMI accident were caused by people, not equipment. They felt operators needed to receive better training and not rely so much on equipment. They went on to say,

We are convinced that if the only problems were equipment problems, this Presidential Commission would never have been created. The equipment was sufficiently good that, except for human failures, the major accident at Three Mile Island would have been a minor incident. But, wherever we looked, we found problems with the human beings who operate the plant, with the management that runs the key organization, and with the agency that is charged with assuring the safety of nuclear power plants.[10]

Still Uncertain

Even with the immediate crisis resolved, people who lived in the vicinity of TMI would still wonder if they had received doses of radiation. Many of the health effects of radiation, such as cancer, are not obvious for years. This uncertainty was best summed up by a T-shirt slogan: "I Survived Three Mile Island . . . I Think."[11]

While the crisis had passed and life was returning
to normal in the towns near Three Mile Island, the
presidential commission still raised many questions.
Those questions, along with the public's tarnished
opinion about nuclear energy, would change the
nuclear industry.

*Denton, left, testifies for the President's Commission on the Accident
at Three Mile Island.*

Technicians protect themselves before entering the containment building during the cleanup stage after the damaged reactor was shut down.

THE LEGACY OF THREE MILE ISLAND

With the immediate crisis over, the next step was to bring TMI-2 to what is called a cold shutdown. This happens when all the water in the cooling system has a temperature below the boiling point. This finally happened on

April 27, 1979. TMI-2 was now completely out of danger. Its reactor would never be restarted. But this was only the beginning. Accident cleanup would take many years and huge amounts of money. Metropolitan Edison had already been fined $155,000 for mismanagement during the accident. However, it would take $1 billion and 13 years to complete the cleanup.

It was during the cleanup phase, in the summer of 1982, when operators lowered a camera into the reactor and were able to see the core and fuel rods for the first time since the accident:

> *At a depth of 5 feet (1.3 meters) below the top of where the fuel should have been, the camera revealed distinguishable parts of the reactor sitting on a coarse bed of gravel and debris. A third of the core had been damaged and a large void had formed that was filled only by coolant water. What had happened to the fuel was not clear and would not be known fully for several more years, but one thing was perfectly obvious: the accident had been severe and the core damaged beyond repair.*[1]

They would later find that between nine and ten short tons (8 and 9 metric tons) of fuel had melted and flowed into the lower part of the reactor.

Eventually, the fuel was removed from the reactor vessel and shipped to the Idaho National Engineering Laboratory in special casks for storage. The fuel that could not be removed was left at TMI in safe storage and remains there still. While TMI-1 is still operating, nothing more than monitoring will be done with TMI-2. Once TMI-1 is decommissioned, or no longer used, both plants will be disassembled.

Lasting Effects

As of yet, no lasting health effects have been documented as a result of the TMI accident. But the accident did have a huge effect on the US nuclear industry, which came to a standstill. While existing plants continue operating, no new plants have been approved since the 1979 accident. Plans for new plants have been scrapped or put on indefinite hold for almost 30 years. However,

Decommissioning

Decommissioning is the process of taking a nuclear power plant out of service. The NRC designates three types of decommissioning: DECON, SAFESTOR, and ENTOMB. DECON involves taking a plant down immediately and removing any radioactive materials. SAFESTOR is similar, except that the plant is first allowed to sit long enough for some radioactivity to decay, which usually takes years. ENTOMB involves encasing any radioactive elements in concrete and monitoring them until the radioactivity level decreases.

interest in nuclear energy has grown in recent years because of the need to lessen the United States' dependence on foreign energy sources. There have been applications for 30 new nuclear plants since 2007, but the 2011 earthquake and tsunami in Japan, which resulted in severe damage to several nuclear plants, may once again make Americans reluctant to build new nuclear power plants.

There have also been changes in the industry itself, due to the accident. In late

Transporting Nuclear Waste

During the cleanup phase, contaminated fuel was removed from the TMI-2 reactor vessel and shipped to the Idaho National Engineering Laboratory, where it would be stored. But how can radioactive fuel move safely all the way from Pennsylvania to Idaho? Most radioactive cargo is encased in special casks and transported by truck. The packaging and transportation are highly regulated, and the truck drivers are specially trained. The truck route is planned according to federal highway regulations, which include avoiding large cities.

The containers that hold the radioactive material are made from steel lined with lead shielding. These containers have been tested and can withstand traffic accidents, fire, and water. They have been dropped onto steel rods, run into concrete walls, and dropped onto concrete from a height of 2,000 feet (600 m). One test even included hitting a container broadside with a rocket-assisted, 120-short ton (108-metric ton) locomotive train traveling 80 miles an hour (128 km/h). In every test, the containers remained intact.

And while some people worry about contamination from radioactive waste traveling through their town, there is little cause for fear. Those residents actually receive more radiation eating a banana than they would watching a year's worth of nuclear shipments pass by.

1979, in response to the president's commission report about the NRC's failings, the nuclear industry created the Institute of Nuclear Power Operations (INPO). INPO's purpose is to create and monitor new guidelines for nuclear plant training and operation. It closely monitors and inspects power plants and their training programs. INPO makes sure nuclear plant operators have proper skills and knowledge so they no longer have to rely just on the safety equipment in their plants.

In 1985, also in response to the events at Three Mile Island, the Federal Radiological Monitoring and Assessment Center (FRMAC) formed. Its purpose is to coordinate the information and data received during a nuclear emergency and share it with state and local governments. According to current administrator Thomas D'Agostino,

Human Guinea Pigs?

Many people who lived near TMI at the time of the accident feel like human guinea pigs. Their health is monitored to learn more about the long-term effects of low-level doses of radiation. There has been some evidence of slightly increased rates of cancer among people in the TMI area, as well as some babies born after the accident who had thyroid problems, but no official study has yet been published.

An NRC instructor performs an emergency drill on a simulator,
demonstrating the improved training required
for nuclear plant technicians.

The Center is a prime example of our investment in nuclear security providing the United States with the tools to tackle broad national challenges. For 25 years, FRMAC has provided the nation the unparalleled ability to respond to radiological emergencies with a quick, coordinated response across federal, state, and local agencies in the event of an emergency.[2]

As a result of TMI, the nuclear industry has become safer and more reliable. However, the accident also increased the number of groups and individuals opposed to nuclear power. People who were already against nuclear power became more so after the accident. Their general fears about nuclear energy had become a real and frightening event. In addition, many people who previously thought nuclear energy was a good alternate source of energy began to oppose it after the accident.

30 Years Later

March 28, 2009, marked the thirtieth anniversary of the accident at Three Mile Island. While previous anniversaries were mostly noted with more protests against nuclear energy, this anniversary showed that more people were in favor of nuclear energy than before. A Gallup poll showed 59 percent of those polled

Radiation Protection Limits

What are safe levels of radiation exposure? Historically, the limit for radiation exposure for the general public was 500 millirems a year. Today, the yearly limit for the public has been lowered to 100 millirems. The limit for occupational exposure, such as for those working in nuclear plants, is 5,000 millirems a year. Some recent studies have suggested, however, that health problems can possibly develop even at this occupational rate.

were in favor of nuclear power—the highest percentage since the TMI accident. However, while people once feared a nuclear accident at a power plant, today many people fear a terrorist action on a power plant.

As Americans seek new energy sources in an effort to be less dependent on foreign sources such as oil and to be more environmentally friendly, nuclear power is once again a serious option. As Pennsylvania Governor Ed Rendell noted in the article "Three Mile Island's 30th Anniversary Sees Nuclear Renaissance,"

> By no means is (nuclear power) the sole answer to our energy problems, but I think it actually has a definitive place in the whole array of things we need to do to reach our goals of producing enough [energy] to meet demand.[3]

But TMI has left a legacy of mistrust that some people have

Murphy's Law

Reporter Mike Gray commented on the aftermath of the TMI accident: "Many of these plants identical to Three Mile Island are still in operation. There is no question that the Nuclear Regulatory Commission learned something from this accident and they no longer have the cavalier attitude about plant safety that they did in 1979. It's not that another accident could happen, but that it almost certainly will happen because, as Murphy's Law dictates, if something can go wrong, it will."[4]

learned to live with and yet others are still bothered by. Ann Trunk, who lives in Middletown, served as a member of the President's Commission on the Accident at Three Mile Island. "I think there is still an element of people who are frightened by nuclear power," she noted. "I don't think people have changed their minds that much." As for the people who are not frightened, she explained, "I won't say they're apathetic, but TMI is there, and so what? We've learned to live. Some people are comfortable."[5]

Decades later, Three Mile Island still affects public opinion about using nuclear power to meet the nation's increased energy demands.

TIMELINE

March 28, 1979

At approximately 4:00 a.m., the feedwater pump in the TMI-2 reactor stops, and the turbine stops.

March 28

Roughly three to six seconds later, pressure in the primary system reaches critical level, and the pressurizer relief valve opens.

March 28

The reactor scrams approximately six seconds after the valve opens.

March 28

By approximately 6:48 a.m., radiation levels increase in the auxiliary and reactor buildings.

March 28

A site emergency is declared shortly before 7:00 a.m.

March 29, 1979

Governor Thornburgh is informed at approximately 11:00 p.m. that there is damage to the reactor core at TMI-2.

March 28	March 28	March 28
The coolant drain tank relief valve opens at approximately 4:03 a.m., spilling coolant into the reactor building basement.	At 4:04 a.m., an operator reduces the emergency cooling system; he shuts down the last emergency pump approximately one minute later.	Contaminated water is pumped from the reactor building to the auxiliary building at approximately 4:08 a.m.

March 30, 1979	March 30	March 30
Around 8:00 a.m., radioactive material is released from TMI-2.	A hydrogen bubble is detected inside the reactor vessel at approximately 11:30 a.m.	Due to the release of radioactive material, an evacuation order is given at 12:30 p.m. for young children and pregnant women.

TIMELINE

March 31, 1979	April 1, 1979	April 9, 1979
A press conference is held to reassure the public that the hydrogen bubble is shrinking and an explosion is not possible.	President and First Lady Carter arrive at TMI.	The crisis is officially declared over.

October 30, 1979	1982	1985
The President's Commission on the Accident at Three Mile Island presents its findings.	Cameras give the first view inside the damaged reactor core.	Defueling the reactor officially begins in October.

April 11, 1979

President Carter creates a presidential commission to study the TMI accident.

April 27, 1979

The reactor reaches cold shutdown.

October 25, 1979

The NRC fines Met-Ed $155,000 for mismanagement of the crisis.

1990

Defueling TMI-2 is completed in January.

1993

In December, TMI-2 is placed in monitored storage status.

ESSENTIAL FACTS

DATE OF EVENT

March 28–April 9, 1979

PLACE OF EVENT

Three Mile Island Nuclear Power Plant, Middletown, Pennsylvania

KEY PLAYERS

❖ Lieutenant Governor William Scranton

❖ Governor Richard Thornburgh

❖ NRC officials Harold Denton and Joseph Hendrie

❖ President Jimmy Carter

❖ Metropolitan Edison

❖ Nuclear Regulatory Commission

Highlights of Event

❖ Due to a faulty feedwater pump, problems with cooling water valves, and some human error, the reactor at the TMI-2 nuclear plant overheated. Some fuel did melt down, and some radiation was released into the atmosphere.

❖ After a miscommunication about a radiation-level reading two days after the accident, the governor's office and the NRC gave an evacuation order for young children and pregnant women living near the plant. Despite the perimeters of the order, most locals—approximately 144,000—evacuated during the crisis.

❖ As a turning point, President Jimmy Carter toured TMI-2 four days after the accident to learn more about the resolving crisis and bolster public confidence in surrounding communities as well as nationwide.

❖ It took 13 years and $1 billion to clean and decommission the damaged plant. No new nuclear power plants have been approved in the United States since 1979, even though the US nuclear industry has increased safety measures in response to the accident.

Quote

"Never before have people been asked to live with such ambiguity. The TMI accident—an accident we cannot see or taste or smell . . . is an accident that is invisible. I think the fact that it is invisible creates a sense of uncertainty and fright on the part of people that may well go beyond the reality of the accident itself."—*Theodore Gross, Pennsylvania State University provost, speaking to the presidential commission about the toll of the Three Mile Island accident*

Glossary

atom
The smallest part of an element that still retains the characteristics of that element.

cladding
The outer metallic jacket on a fuel rod.

contamination
The presence of unwanted radioactive materials on surfaces, structures, or objects.

control rod
A device made from neutron-absorbing material, used to regulate the nuclear reaction inside the core.

core
The part of a nuclear reactor that contains nuclear fuel.

fossil fuels
Substances such as oil, petroleum, and natural gas that are made of hydrocarbons and are used for fuel.

meltdown
When a nuclear reactor overheats, melting its fuel rods and causing the release of radioactive materials and radiation.

millirem
One-thousandth of a rem.

nuclear power
A type of energy that comes from particles found in atoms.

nuclear reactor
A piece of equipment where a nuclear reaction can be started, maintained, and controlled, generating energy.

radioactivity
Radiation emitted by a nuclear reaction.

reactor vessel
The structure that contains the nuclear reactor and keeps radiation from escaping.

scram
The rapid shutdown of a nuclear reactor, usually done by inserting the control rods.

steam generator
A heat exchanger where heat from one coolant loop is transferred to a second coolant loop, causing the water to boil and creating steam.

turbine
A machine with blades driven by steam, which produces electricity.

uranium
An element extracted from certain minerals and used as nuclear fuel.

utility
A business organization, such as an electric, water, or power company, that provides a public service and is regulated by the government.

ADDITIONAL RESOURCES

SELECTED BIBLIOGRAPHY

"Backgrounder on the Three Mile Island Accident." *United States Nuclear Regulatory Commission*. NRC, 15 Mar. 2011. Web. 20 Jul. 2011.

Osif, Bonnie A., et al. *TMI 25 Years Later: The Three Mile Island Nuclear Power Plant Accident and Its Impact*. University Park, PA: Pennsylvania State UP, 2004. Print.

Walker, J. Samuel. *Three Mile Island: A Nuclear Crisis in Historical Perspective*. Berkeley, CA: U of California P, 2004. Print.

FURTHER READINGS

Hampton, Wilborn. *Meltdown: A Race Against Nuclear Disaster at Three Mile Island: A Reporter's Story*. New York: Candlewick, 2001. Print.

Lusted, Marcia Amidon, and Greg Lusted. *Building History: A Nuclear Power Plant*. Farmington Hills, MI: Lucent, 2005. Print.

Lusted, Marcia Amidon. *Essential Events: The Chernobyl Disaster*. Edina, MN: Abdo, 2011. Print.

Web Links

To learn more about Three Mile Island, visit ABDO Publishing Company online at **www.abdopublishing.com**. Web sites about Three Mile Island are featured on our Book Links page. These links are routinely monitored and updated to provide the most current information available.

Places to Visit

Bradbury Science Museum
1350 Central Avenue, Los Alamos, NM 87544
http://www.lanl.gov/museum
The museum is part of the Los Alamos National Laboratory (LANL), one of the nation's top developers and researchers for nuclear weaponry and other national security matters. The museum educates visitors about LANL's history as well as its current research.

Harris Nuclear Power Plant Energy and Environmental Center
New Hill-Holleman Road, New Hill, NC 27562
919-362-3261
Located near the Harris nuclear power plant, the center offers hands-on exhibits about nuclear power, electricity, and alternative energy.

National Museum of Nuclear Science and History
601 Eubank Blvd SE, Albuquerque, NM 87123
http://www.nuclearmuseum.org
A congressionally chartered museum, its exhibits cover the history of nuclear development and the future of nuclear technology for peaceful uses.

Three Mile Island Nuclear Power Plant
Route 441S PO Box 480, Middletown, Pennsylvania 17057
http://www.exeloncorp.com/powerplants/threemileisland/
The visitors center features exhibits and video displays about nuclear energy and the Three Mile Island plant.

Source Notes

Chapter 1. March 28, 1979

1. Laurence Stern, et al. "Crisis at Three Mile Island." *Washington Post*. Washington Post, 1999. Web. 29 July 2011.

2. "American Experience: Meltdown at Three Mile Island." *PBS*. WGBH Educational Foundation, 1999. Web. 29 July 2011.

3. John G. Kemeny, et al. *Report of the President's Commission on The Accident at Three Mile Island*. Washington DC: US Government Printing Office, 1979. Print. 91.

4. Laurence Stern, et al. "Crisis at Three Mile Island." *Washington Post*. Washington Post, 1999. Web. 29 July 2011.

5. John G. Kemeny, et al. *Report of the President's Commission on The Accident at Three Mile Island*. Washington DC: US Government Printing Office, 1979. Print. 81.

6. "American Experience: Meltdown at Three Mile Island." *PBS*. WGBH Educational Foundation, 1999. Web. 29 July 2011.

7. Laurence Stern, et al. "Crisis at Three Mile Island." *Washington Post*. Washington Post, 1999. Web. 29 July 2011.

8. "American Experience: Meltdown at Three Mile Island." *PBS*. WGBH Educational Foundation, 1999. Web. 29 July 2011.

Chapter 2. Nuclear Power in the United States

1. Robert Martin. "The History of Nuclear Power Plant Safety: The Forties." *American Nuclear Society Public Information Committee*. American Nuclear Society, n.d. Web. 29 July 2011.

2. Dwight D. Eisenhower. "Atoms for Peace." *International Atomic Energy Agency*. International Atomic Energy Agency, n.d. Web. 29 July 2011.

3. Robert Martin. "The History of Nuclear Power Plant Safety: The Fifties." *American Nuclear Society Public Information Committee*. American Nuclear Society, n.d. Web. 29 July 2011.

Chapter 3. How a Nuclear Plant Works

1. *Nuclear Power: Answers to Your Questions*. Washington, DC: Edison Electric Institute, 1988. Print. 30.

Chapter 4. Emergency

1. Laurence Stern, et al. "Crisis at Three Mile Island." *Washington Post*. Washington Post, 1999. Web. 29 July 2011.

2. Ibid.

3. J. Samuel Walker. *Three Mile Island: A Nuclear Crisis in Historical Perspective*. Berkeley, CA: U of California P, 2004. Print. 77.

4. Ibid. 83.

5. John G. Kemeny, et al. *Report of the President's Commission on The Accident at Three Mile Island*. Washington DC: US Government Printing Office, 1979. Print. 103–104.

6. "Three Mile Island Unit 2: 1979–2008." *Three Mile Island Alert*. Three Mile Island Alert, 2009. Web. 29 July 2011.

7. "American Experience: Meltdown at Three Mile Island." *PBS*. WGBH Educational Foundation, 1999. Web. 29 July 2011.

Chapter 5. March 29, 1979

1. John G. Kemeny, et al. *Report of the President's Commission on The Accident at Three Mile Island*. Washington DC: US Government Printing Office, 1979. Print. 111.

2. J. Samuel Walker. *Three Mile Island: A Nuclear Crisis in Historical Perspective*. Berkeley, CA: U of California P, 2004. Print. 107.

3. "American Experience: Meltdown at Three Mile Island." *PBS*. WGBH Educational Foundation, 1999. Web. 29 July 2011.

4. J. Samuel Walker. *Three Mile Island: A Nuclear Crisis in Historical Perspective*. Berkeley, CA: U of California P, 2004. Print. 108.

5. John G. Kemeny, et al. *Report of the President's Commission on The Accident at Three Mile Island*. Washington DC: US Government Printing Office, 1979. Print. 111.

6. J. Samuel Walker. *Three Mile Island: A Nuclear Crisis in Historical Perspective*. Berkeley, CA: U of California P, 2004. Print. 103.

7. John G. Kemeny, et al. *Report of the President's Commission on The Accident at Three Mile Island*. Washington DC: US Government Printing Office, 1979. Print. 115.

Source Notes Continued

Chapter 6. March 30, 1979

1. Bonnie A. Osif, Anthony J. Baratta, and Thomas W. Conkling. *TMI 25 Years Later: The Three Mile Island Nuclear Power Plant Accident and Its Impact*. University Park, PA: Pennsylvania State UP, 2004. Print. 29.

2. "American Experience: Meltdown at Three Mile Island." *PBS*. WGBH Educational Foundation, 1999. Web. 29 July 2011.

3. J. Samuel Walker. *Three Mile Island: A Nuclear Crisis in Historical Perspective*. Berkeley, CA: U of California P, 2004. Print. 126.

4. Ibid. 138.

5. Ibid. 133.

6. "American Experience: Meltdown at Three Mile Island." *PBS*. WGBH Educational Foundation, 1999. Web. 29 July 2011.

Chapter 7. The Hydrogen Bubble

1. Laurence Stern, et al. "Crisis at Three Mile Island." *Washington Post*. Washington Post, 1999. Web. 29 July 2011.

2. "American Experience: Meltdown at Three Mile Island." *PBS*. WGBH Educational Foundation, 1999. Web. 29 July 2011.

3. J. Samuel Walker. *Three Mile Island: A Nuclear Crisis in Historical Perspective*. Berkeley, CA: U of California P, 2004. Print. 142.

4. Laurence Stern, et al. "Crisis at Three Mile Island." *Washington Post*. Washington Post, 1999. Web. 29 July 2011.

5. Ibid.

Chapter 8. The Crisis Resolved

1. Laurence Stern, et al. "Crisis at Three Mile Island." *Washington Post*. Washington Post, 1999. Web. 29 July 2011.

2. Ibid.

3. Ibid.

4. Ibid.

5. "American Experience: Meltdown at Three Mile Island." *PBS*. WGBH Educational Foundation, 1999. Web. 29 July 2011.

6. Laurence Stern, et al. "Crisis at Three Mile Island." *Washington Post*. Washington Post, 1999. Web. 29 July 2011.

7. John G. Kemeny, et al. *Report of the President's Commission on The Accident at Three Mile Island*. Washington DC: US Government Printing Office, 1979. Print. 135.

8. Laurence Stern, et al. "Crisis at Three Mile Island." *Washington Post*. Washington Post, 1999. Web. 29 July 2011.

9. John G. Kemeny, et al. *Report of the President's Commission on The Accident at Three Mile Island*. Washington DC: US Government Printing Office, 1979. Print. 7.

10. Ibid. 8.

11. J. Samuel Walker. *Three Mile Island: A Nuclear Crisis in Historical Perspective*. Berkeley, CA: U of California P, 2004. Print. 208.

Chapter 9. The Legacy of Three Mile Island

1. Bonnie A. Osif, Anthony J. Baratta, and Thomas W. Conkling. *TMI 25 Years Later: The Three Mile Island Nuclear Power Plant Accident and Its Impact*. University Park, PA: Pennsylvania State UP, 2004. Print. 41.

2. "NNSA Celebrates 25th Anniversary of Federal Radiological Monitoring and Assessment Center." *National Nuclear Security Administration*. US Department of Energy, 23 November 2010. Web. 29 July 2011.

3. Marc Levy. "Three Mile Island's 30th Anniversary Sees Nuclear Renaissance." *Huffington Post*. Huffington Post, 26 March 2009. Web. 29 July 2011.

4. "American Experience: Meltdown at Three Mile Island." *PBS*. WGBH Educational Foundation, 1999. Web. 29 July 2011.

5. Laurence Stern, et al. "Crisis at Three Mile Island." *Washington Post*. Washington Post, 1999. Web. 29 July 2011.

INDEX

About the Author

Marcia Amidon Lusted is the author of more than 50 books and many magazine articles for young readers. She is also an assistant editor for Cobblestone Publishing, a writing instructor, and a musician. She lives in New Hampshire.

Photo Credits